Thrilling Your Customers

How To Increase Sales for Your Small Business by Creating Genuine Customer Connections

By D.J. Billings

Table of Contents

Introduction

Do you like people?

This is a book about people. It's not about tactics or tricks, it's not about gaming your way out of customer service issues. It's about serving people. So I have to ask: *Do you like people?*

I don't mean tolerating them, or seeing them as a thing you are resigned to deal with. I mean, do you genuinely like other humans? It's okay if you don't. It's 100% fine if you aren't what some call a "people person." If other humans turn you into Ebeneezer Scrooge, then that's just you. It's important to be honest with yourself.

Maybe you like people well enough, but you're sort of an introvert and the thought of multiple interactions daily makes you break out in hives. You're not alone. If you can come to terms with your introvertedness, you'll be in a much better place to manage your business.

If you've come to either of these realizations, don't panic. You can still learn how to give great customer service and stay true to who you are. Even if you decide that you don't want to deal with customers directly, this book will help you train other people to keep your customers happy and overjoyed with the service they receive.

If you already like people and you can handle lots of interaction, then you have a head start on helping them in a way that also helps your business. You may have customer service problems, you may have anxiety about dealing with your customers, you may be wondering why your customers aren't coming back, but those problems are all solvable. You can do this. I promise.

I've been working in some capacity of customer service since I was in my early teens. I've dealt with every kind of customer you could encounter, from movie theater patrons to air travelers and even high-level attorneys. Today I run multiple businesses where I work with both easy customers and challenging customers every day.

Over the years I've found that truly great customer service is not about manipulation or one-upping your customers. If you're looking for a shortcut to scamming people or trying to outwit Yelp reviewers, this isn't the book for you. This is a book about being of service.

It's not difficult to learn how to handle customers in a way that thrills them and keeps them coming back, but there are some secrets you may not know. I'm going to explain them to you and you'll come away with an inspired sense of how to work with all types of people in any business, in a way that increases your sales and will help your business keep going for the long term.

In my businesses, more often than not, my customers not only thank me, but leave with hugs and smiles. Some have even become very good friends. If you think that's impossible for you, then this book will change your mind. I'm going to show you how to make it happen.

Let's get started!

Chapter One

Why Brick and Mortar Is Dying

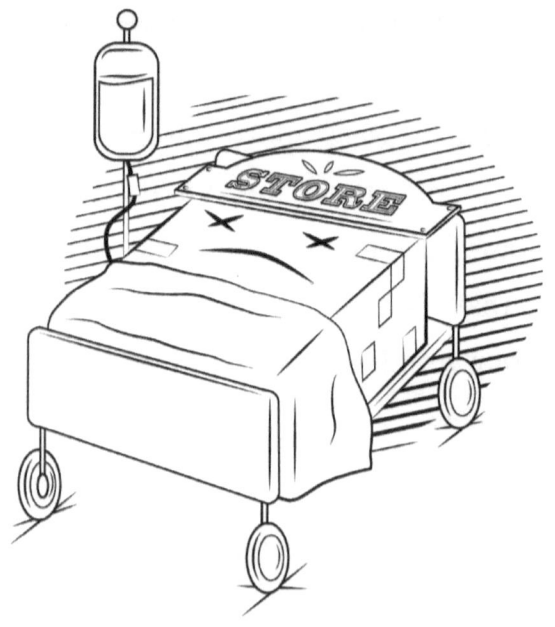

We hear the sad stories in the news almost every day. Sometimes we even see it for ourselves when we visit the local mall or drive down what used to be a busy shopping street that is now plastered with For Lease signs instead of shop names. Windows are dark and dusty, no one is cleaning up the trash anymore.

More homeless people are camping out in storefronts. It's like that scene from Back to the Future II where Marty McFly ends up in a nightmarish, alternate future. Except that it's actually starting to happen in the real world, and brick and mortar retail stores really are dying.

Why is this happening? Many business owners and the media are quick to blame Amazon and ecommerce. While that may be one part of the puzzle, we need to look deeper. Let's jump into the Wayback Machine and look at some history.

Video Killed the Cinema Star

Back in the 1980s when video stores started to spring up and the VCR was becoming affordable for middle-class families, the big movie studios were in a panic. Several of them got together and actually lobbied the U.S. government to put a stop to it. They were spooked by these little video stores. They were sure that families watching movies at home on the couch would destroy cinema. Spoiler alert: It didn't happen. Video stores eventually died out anyway. These days we've swapped tape and DVD rentals for

Netflix and other streaming channels. Yet even with the popularity of those platforms, millions of people still go to movie theaters to watch new films.

Panic at the Costco

Like the movie studios forty years ago, retailers are in a similar panic right now with the threat of ecommerce. Amazon started doing business in 1994 and is currently the leader in ecommerce. While other big box stores like Target, WalMart and Barnes & Noble also have ecommerce sites, Amazon is different because it has no brick and mortar location. They make it easy to avoid the freeways, parking, and the lines. Customers can even get their item delivered the same day – often at cheaper prices than the store down the street. That's hard for a big box store to beat, let alone a mom-and-pop retail shop.

It seems that ecommerce, especially Amazon, is easy to blame for the failure of Main Street and mall stores. The general feeling is that if you can't compete with Amazon, it's an unfair situation and you're doomed to fail.

That is a cop out.

Retail stores trying to compete with Amazon's ease of buying and inhumanly fast delivery are missing out on the one thing that Amazon can't compete on: connection, both human and environment.

On the Internet, No One Can Smell Your Books

When was the last time you bought a book? Was it online or at a local bookstore? If you're a book lover, you know that part of the appeal is taking down a book and feeling the weight in your hands. The smell of the paper and ink are visceral. If it's a little musty, that's a bonus. Especially in used book stores, there's a sense of history and story that we don't get from a computer screen. Who owned this book before? When you see an inside cover inscribed, "To Daniel, 1977," the mystery of who Daniel is and who gifted him the book becomes as much a part of the story as the actual tale the author wrote.

People who love books love being surrounded by them. It's impossible for a book lover to pass any kind of bookstore and not stop, even if only for a moment. That's powerful.

I'm Only Human, of Flesh and Blood I'm Made

And what about the people? It's ironic, but the more retail stores replace people to make service faster, the more they start losing out to ecommerce. Self-checkouts are becoming ubiquitous. It may be streamlining the shopping experience, making checkout more efficient, but there's something missing. Customers shopping retail, or going to a theater or a restaurant still expect some kind of human interaction. Having humans in a shop can be comforting. Amazon and other ecommerce stores can't offer that. I truly believe that in the end, people will choose human interaction over convenience.

To flip the original question of this chapter to the more actionable, we should ask: How can we keep brick and mortar stores alive?

It's Different for Shops

First, stop trying to compete. That doesn't mean giving up and letting Amazon win. In fact, this is a very positive step to take, because once you eliminate the stress of trying to keep up with Amazon, you can take better, more thoughtful steps to make your own store uniquely valuable.

You can still do your own version of online business. It's not only a great idea, these days customers actually expect you to have at least a website. So why not expand your reach by offering products online through Amazon Marketplace, Etsy or other established stores? Leverage their power to grow your business. Just don't try to imitate their models.

Be a Racehorse – Er, Resource

If you have a physical location run by humans, you have a huge advantage. There's a lot you can do to bring in people that isn't limited to only selling products or services. You can host workshops, give free demonstrations, provide information that relates to your business that's truly helpful to potential customers. When people keep coming back to your store because you're a resource, they will eventually buy and even better, bring their friends.

This is also true if you operate at farmer's markets, events or pop-ups. You can still create an environment that engages people and gets them interacting, rather than looking at yet another table of stuff to buy.

Similarly, you can create events where your local community members can participate. Join your local Chamber of Commerce and offer to host events at your location. If you're a bookseller, host signings or encourage customers to have their book club at your shop. Serve tea and cookies (free of charge) to the group.

If you make your business a local resource and not just a place to buy more stuff, you will create something that people will actively choose over ecommerce every time.

Create an Environment for Interaction

You have a very special opportunity every time a customer visits your store. You can engage in conversations with them, which is something they can't get when shopping from their keyboard. I'll get into this in more detail in a later section, but for the moment just ponder the notion that every time a human being enters your store, you already start with an advantage over ecommerce. What you do with that opportunity is up to you, and we'll get into more depth on this so you have actionable steps you can take.

Again, when I say "store," I am also including pop-ups, farmer's markets and other events. This is important because even though your locations are temporary, you can create these environments and experiences that people love.

Online Sellers Still Have Hope

Even if you only sell online, you can still take away some valuable lessons from this chapter. Although you don't have real people walking into a space with whom you can interact, there are still great opportunities to create connections with potential customers. The same principles this book that apply to brick and mortar apply to online stores as well.

Think of social media and email as your physical space. In those platforms you can interact with people from all over the world with almost non-existent overhead.

Consider selling at a local market or event where you can meet people face to face. Even if your sales at the event are low, you are still creating a huge opportunity for potential customers to know you and find you online.

Being small actually gives you a major advantage over Amazon and other big ecommerce retailers. Embrace being small. It's a gift, really. Use your magical powers of personal connection to bring people in to your space, whether it's online, in a shop or a tent at a market.

Chapter Two

Communication Secrets

Do you want to know a little secret? There's something that every human being and most other creatures on this planet want and need on a regular basis. No, it's not love, although this could be considered a form of it.

It's acknowledgement.

Not the kind you get when you win an award or get a diploma, it's more like when you know that you are truly being seen and heard. It's really powerful.

Think about a time when you were waiting in a long line for something, so long you couldn't even see the end. You've been standing for more than 15 minutes with no movement. You and the people around you are getting edgy. Everyone is thinking the same things. *How long will this take? Are we ever going to move at all? Does anyone even know we're here? Does anyone care? Is this worth it?*

Suddenly, an employee starts walking up the line and every once in a while stops to talk to a group of people waiting. When they get to you they say, "Sorry, Folks, I know you've been waiting a while here. We were experiencing a technical difficulty but we should be getting you in very soon. We should have you all inside in about ten minutes."

Everyone breathes a little easier. Ten more minutes isn't so bad. At least now you know what's up. Sure enough, the line starts moving slowly and you can see yourself making it inside.

The difference in having an edgy, impatient crowd and a relaxed one is in the communication. It started with the employee acknowledging that they knew you had been waiting and that wasn't how it was supposed to go. It sounds simple, but it's huge. Simple and clear acknowledgement can change the mood of one customer or a whole crowd in a moment. It can be the difference between a mob and a quiet line.

If I were to tell you one thing to change in your customer service, this is it. No matter what kind of business you have and no matter how you're communicating with them, you need to start practicing acknowledgement right now. Here are a few ways:

In-person Greeting

I'll get more into this in a later chapter, but simply saying "Hello" when someone comes into your space makes a big difference. It tells them that you see them, you know they are there and you're welcoming them. If you're busy with another customer, chances are they get it, so just saying hello helps them feel acknowledged before you can do anything else.

Return the Call

Realistically, we can't always answer the phone. That's totally okay, it's why they invented voicemail. If you don't have your voicemail system set up, then stop reading this and go take of that right now.

When you get a voicemail, you need to return the call (unless they said it wasn't necessary, of course. Use your judgment). Maybe this sounds obvious, but there are people out there who have unreturned voicemails stacked up. If that's you, you need to change that.

Sometimes it won't matter that you don't actually call them back on the phone. If you text, send an email or if you're in contact on social media, that can work fine. You're still returning their call. The point is that you're acknowledging that they wanted to get in touch with you. So even if you don't have an answer for them or don't know how to help them right off the bat, you need to contact them back and make sure they know you've heard them.

Email

Email sucks. We all know it. We all deal with it. When you're running a small business, it may be a necessary evil but it's also an amazing communication tool.

Just like with returning calls, you absolutely must answer email inquiries. If someone is reaching out to your business, it's called a lead. If you let that lead die, you may as well lock your doors so people can't get in. It's just as bad. Answer emails and answer them promptly. Again, it's okay if you don't have every answer or solution all tied up in a neat little digital bow. You can simply respond to let them know that you got their email and you're working on an answer. It's exactly like the line, and this is why many tech support responses start out with an email just to say they saw your request and are working it. Brilliant.

Try to answer emails promptly. You don't have to monitor your Gmail app on your phone during dinner (that's bad for your other relationships). Set an internal policy for responding, like "I'll answer very email within 24 hours," and stick to it. If you have so many emails flooding your inbox that it's getting impossible, then you need to hire an assistant to simply be your Acknowledger (which incidentally is a good problem to have).

The principle applies no matter what method of communication you use. Texting, social media, online orders, it's all the same. Acknowledgment is your mantra.

This Person Is Repeating on Me

Have you ever been on a tech support call or chat where they repeat every single thing you say? It goes like this:

YOU: My internet is not working.

CSR: Okay, I hear that your internet is not working, I will help you with that. Is it plugged in?

YOU: Yes, it's plugged in.

CSR: Thank you, it is plugged in. Is the light blinking?

YOU: No, the light's not blinking.

CSR: Okay, the light is not blinking.

YOU: Stop repeating my words, just tell me how to fix it!

CSR: Okay, I will stop repeating your words and just tell you how to fix it.

YOU: AAAARRGGGHHHH!!!

If you're not tearing your hair out by now, then you have superhuman patience. Sure, part of acknowledgment can include repeating back what a customer says to make sure you're clear and that they know you've heard them. If you take it too far, it will have the opposite effect. They'll think you're just taking notes and not really understanding what they need.

Bottom Line Time

Just be human. Have yourself a regular ol' conversation and make sure you listen. It's really very simple.

Chapter Three

Your Sales and Marketing Should Be Baked in

Every single person in your business who interacts with customers in any way is in sales and marketing. You may have heard this before, and that's because it's absolutely true. In your business you may designate specific salespeople or have a dedicated marketing team, but you must realize that you are all responsible for both marketing and sales.

It's Not the Money, Honey

It's crucially important to understand that sales is not merely a transaction of goods or services for money. Sales is a transaction of human feeling. Money changes hands and your customer receives something they wanted or needed, but what they take away is the feeling they got from the experience. This is so important, I'll repeat it: Sales is a transaction of human feeling. There are no exceptions to this!

To show you how this works, let me send you on a little trip to get some coffee (it's on me). Here's how it goes. You walk in the door and it's moderately busy, people behind the counter are either taking orders or making drinks. While you wait in line, someone is sweeping the floor and they sweep right over your feet without acknowledging you. When you get to the counter, the clerk looks tired, grumpy and robotically mumbles, "Welcome to Grinder Schminder, may I take your order?" So you explain that you want a regular coffee, but with steamed soy milk, no foam. "So you want, like, a latte." they correct you. You explain your order again and they shrug. "Is that all?" they ask. "It'll be at the end of the counter."

You get your drink, and sure enough, it's a latte. So you get back in line and tell the clerk that you got the wrong drink and they sigh and say they'll have a new one made for you. It comes up at the end of the counter and now it's correct. You head out of the shop.

How do you feel about your drink? Are you enjoying it? Is it as satisfying as you imagined or is it kind of a letdown? What are the chances you'll go back to that coffee shop? Will you possibly even tell friends to stay away?

Let's flip this experience around. While you're waiting in line, someone is sweeping. They get to you and stop, say hello, and mention that they have fresh-baked muffin samples at the counter. You get to the counter and try one, and the clerk is ready for you.

"Hi! Oh, I like your earrings, are they little avocados? Cool. What can I get for you?" You explain what you want and they speak it back to you. "Okay, so you just want steamed soy in regular coffee, not a latte, right?" They ask for your name and thank you, letting you know it will be ready for you at the end of the counter. When it's ready, the barista calls your name and confirms your drink order. It's made exactly how you wanted it. They thank you and tell you to have a good day.

Now how do, you feel? Will you go back there again? Will you maybe even tell a friend?

I hope that the difference in these two experiences is obvious. You can't taste the coffee by reading a book, but that doesn't matter. Assuming the coffee quality is the same in both examples, it's about the feeling you had throughout the whole experience.

How does all of this factor into sales and marketing?

It might be tempting to say that the coffee shop already made a sale when you walked in. You wanted coffee, so you found a coffee shop. It's a no-brainer. That may be true. So who was really in "sales" in those situations?

Every single person you interacted with was a salesperson for the coffee shop. Because sales is about connecting with people, every employee in those scenarios had the opportunity to do that. Whether they did or not is the real sale, not merely the money transaction the cashier handled. So it's ultimately a question of whether it was a good sale or a bad sale. Here's what that means.

Sales Is Not a One-Night Stand

A bad sale (like in our first example), means that sure, they pocketed some money and sold a drink, but what feeling did they create in the customer? It was an easy sale because the customer was already coming in prepared to buy a coffee. It seems like there's nothing left to do but collect the money and hand over the drink. An easy sale is not necessarily a good sale. In the first example, it's a bad sale because they very likely ruined the chances of getting future sales from you.

A good sale is about the interaction, not the transaction. In the second example, every person you interacted with when you got your coffee made sure you felt truly welcomed and important, even for brief moments in subtle ways. Even the person sweeping the floor greeted you and interacted in a positive way. It didn't cost the store anything more to create potential future sales, which are very likely.

When you start to treat sales as a long term process, something that goes beyond a single transaction, you'll see your revenue increase.

There are a lot of ways to secure future sales, like posting ads or having an active social media presence. But the best (and least expensive) way to do it is through your customer interactions. Every moment with a customer is an opportunity to make them feel special, so that when they leave they're already thinking about another visit.

This is more difficult with small ecommerce businesses, but it's still possible. For example, you aren't present every time someone buys something from your online store, but you can make sure that they feel welcomed when they get to your site, happy while they shop and appreciated after they purchase something. The long term sales job is to get them to keep coming back for visits. Like in the brick and mortar examples from earlier, think about how your business can be a resource. What can you offer that has value and allows for interaction even without a purchase?

Forget About Sales. Start Helping

When you start out every interaction focused on how much money you'll make, you lose. That kind of short-term thinking is poison to the health of your business.

People can tell when you're only trying to make a quick sale and you don't really care if they get what they need.

The worst thing you can do is to chase down every visitor until a sale is made. It's not The Back Street Boys, it's a customer and you're not trying to get a lock of their hair (unless you own a salon, then go ahead). You need to create an environment where customers feel like they want to hang out for a bit or even come back later (if they feel good, they will). If you or your employees are continually shouting things like "Sweaters are 15% off today!" as soon as someone walks in the door, you're already not listening to what customers are shopping for or need. When you focus on the short term sale, you're losing a huge opportunity to create long term sales.

Similarly, it can be tempting to gather all your employees and train them how you want them to interact with customers. Like a bigger chain store, you can give them prompts so they know exactly how to handle every situation and no one goes "off script." The problem with this approach is that sales becomes a chore for your employees and they feel like they are merely performing for you (and they are). They'll start to lose their natural ability to help people. The result is that customers are half-heartedly greeted in a robotic way. That doesn't foster genuine interactions, and your customers end up feeling like they've got a big dollar sign pinned to their forehead.

Sales is about helping. If you and your employees are genuine in your approach to helping customers find what they need, sales will happen organically. Maybe not in the very moment you'd like them to happen, but eventually they will happen.

The other really bitchin' thing that happens when you start focusing on helping people is that it takes the pressure off of you trying to be all salesy and fake. You're helping someone get what they need. If you have a solution, you show it to them. It's that simple.

The Right People

If you hire the right people, you won't have to create scripts and direct everyone to sell "your" way. So who are the right people? You'll know who they are when you interview them. They're the ones who have an informality and genuineness about them. You naturally like them and if that's how you feel, that's how your customers will probably feel, too. All you need to do is train them in the specifics of their job and let them handle customer interactions themselves. It can be hard to give up that control, but the right people will do the right thing almost every time, without being prompted.

Selling Happiness

One of the best representations of this is Zappos, the online shoe seller. They built their business on providing the best customer service anywhere, "selling happiness." Their customer service model of letting CSRs make decisions about returns without consulting a manager was one of the factors that led them to $1 billion in sales in their first ten years.

Rather than coach your employees on how to make sales, teach them about your products and services so they can provide help to your customers. When you replace "sales" with "helping," your customers will develop trust which can then lead to sales. Even if you send a customer away because what you offered wasn't right for them, they will talk about you and they may very well come back when it is right. That might feel scary, but it works.

~~Sales~~ + Helping = Sales. It's not calculus, but it's a proven formula.

Stop Pushing Me!

"People don't like to be sold, but they love to buy."
– Jeffrey Gitomer

Whether it's over the phone, online or in person, no one likes to feel they are being sold something. Your customers want to be presented with options, to be informed, and to feel they have space to make a decision.

If your salespeople or clerks are pushed to meet quotas and given scripts to follow to ensure that they are always selling, your customers will be turned off.

Here are two examples of the same selling situation. Let's say you're shopping for some wine to serve at dinner that night. You just need one bottle, and you have to get home to get dinner started. While you're browsing, a sales clerk approaches you.

CLERK: Hello, can I help you choose a wine?

YOU: No, thanks. I just need one bottle for tonight and I'm trying to decide between these two.

CLERK: We have a special right now on cases. I can show you some wines over here that you can get for 15% off when you buy the case!

YOU: Thanks, I just need one of these and then I need to get home.

CLERK: It's a really great sale, and if you sign up for our rewards program you can get an additional 5% on a second case!

YOU: I'm not interested, thanks, I really just need to decide on one of these right now.

CLERK: Here, I can sign you up now and you can take the extra 5% at the register. Just fill this out.

YOU: (choosing a wine quickly and walking away) NO, thank you!

Are you as skewed out as I am? Even though the sales clerk may be doing their job by sticking to the sales script, they are not listening to you at all. They may as well be a pre programmed robot. In the end, you're not only annoyed and frustrated at not being left alone to make a decision, the next time you hear about their rewards program (probably at the register), you'll likely be annoyed again. There was no connection being made as people, so the immediate sale suffered, and you're probably going to avoid that employee (or even the store) in the future.

Let's see another way this could go:

CLERK: Hello, can I help you choose a wine?

YOU: No, thanks. I just need one bottle for tonight and I'm trying to decide between these two.

CLERK: Okay. Both are great wines, what are you serving?

YOU: Mushroom risotto and sauteéd broccoli.

CLERK: Oooh, sounds yummy. Can I come? Just kidding. Actually, the one on the left would really compliment the savory mushroom flavor. The other one might be a little too sweet.

YOU: Oh, wow, thanks. I think I'll get this one.

CLERK: No problem. And, I know you're just getting the one bottle, but we do have a special on cases this week if you can make it back.

YOU: Oh, thank you. Maybe I will.

CLERK: Here's a little card so you can check out our rewards program online. It's another 5% off.

YOU: Thanks!

CLERK: Have a good night!

What are the chances you'll not only check out and sign up for the rewards but come back later for the sale on cases? You can see the difference. This time the clerk acknowledged your options, gave you good information, and didn't waste your time with pushy sales scripts. They connected with you as a person, not merely as a quota-filler.

People don't want to be sold but they want to buy. Your customers can tell when you're selling to them and they will put up a little invisible wall that makes it even harder to communicate.

Everyone Is Different

When you have employees who help your customers, whether it's in tech support or selling shoes, you need to realize and embrace the fact that they are all unique individuals. The worst thing you can do is to give everyone the same script to follow. The best thing you can do is to throw the script away and let each person sell in their own way.

Does that sound risky?

When you hire the right people, it's really not. The bigger risk is telling someone who is a natural at sales that they must adhere to your script or selling routine. They'll feel and sound fake and there's a good chance you'll just end up alienating your customers.

When your employees understand your product or service and know what your brand is all about, they'll sell naturally. Give them the tools to make sales, encourage them, offer guidance, but don't give them scripts.

Trader Joe's is a great example of this. They encourage their crew members to be themselves with customers. While they do have suggestions for things to mention about products, the crew members are allowed to do it when and how it feels natural. The result is an easygoing, chatty conversation at checkout that doesn't feel pushy or sales-y.

Sales Is a Marathon, Not a Sprint

Remember that sales are not always immediate. A customer who has a great interaction with you or your staff may not buy in the moment, but they will likely be back. Don't panic every time someone gets off the phone or leaves your store without a sale being transacted. Get used to it. Sales is a marathon, not a sprint.

Chapter Four

When Things Go Wrong
(and They Will)

I want to tell you a little story about how I failed a customer recently, and failed hard. In our screen printing business, we have a very good repeat client who loves our work. She gave us a new design that was really cool. After giving her pricing, she ordered a couple hundred shirts to be printed. It was a bit of a challenge, but I was pretty excited to print this one because I love a great design. When the shirts arrived, I set up the press, painstakingly registered the screens for all the different colors, and got to work.

The prints looked great. I boxed them up and shipped them to our client. I even included a couple of extra items, which is a thing we do regularly and people love it (hint: it also leads to future sales).

The next week I got an email from our client. She was seriously disappointed because the background color on the shirts didn't match the digital design she gave us. Uh oh. She even attached a photo of the shirt and a screen capture from her computer with the design. Sure enough, the background color that I had printed was a bright pink and the original design was a muted lavender. Insert your favorite expletive here.

After I kicked myself (and the desk) for making such a boneheaded mistake, I had to figure out what we were going to do. Once you print a shirt, you can't erase it or clean it off, unfortunately. So that was not an option, no matter how desperately I wanted it to be. I sat down and made a quick list of options we did have:

1. Try to tell her it was kinda close and suggest that hey, maybe her monitor was out of sync.

2. Apologize, explain how distracted I've been lately but promise it will never happen again.

3. Apologize and offer a refund.

4. Apologize, own that I messed up and offer to reprint the order at no charge.

What would you do? Let's go through the thought process behind each option.

In option 1, I'm flat-out lying. I know it's wrong, I can see it's wrong. Better still, so can she. Using option 1 is a cop-out and it's sending our customer the message that we think she's either dumb enough to believe it or passive enough to just accept it. If she wasn't angry before, she would definitely have some justified anger after that response.

In option 2, I'm at least starting with an apology. Then it takes a crazy turn, because why should she care if I've been distracted lately? And what about the promise that it will never happen again? That's lovely, but it has no value whatsoever. She's still stuck with 200 t-shirts that are printed in the wrong color. As for it never happening again, that's a promise that will definitely be fulfilled because the chances of her staying a customer are zero.

Option 3 is much closer to a good solution. However, after she gets her money back what is she going to do? She still needs shirts that are printed correctly. Again, the likelihood of her reinvesting that money with us is slim to none.

It didn't take long for us to settle on option 4. It was really the only solution we felt good offering. I apologized, and when you screw up this should always be the first thing out of your mouth. I owned up to my mistake, which was a hard pill to swallow but it was the truth. There was nothing or no one else to blame, so I didn't try to excuse it or explain it away. Finally, the best thing we could offer was to reprint the order at no charge. Of course, we lost a lot of time and money on this order. We had to buy new blank shirts and start all over again. Not an easy day for our little shop, but we survived and learned a valuable lesson.

So what happened? Well, she accepted our offer and thanked us profusely. Not only that, but she put in an additional order for a different design and other items. So we kept our very good client, she got what she wanted and I lived to print another day.

There are some lessons here that are worth thinking about. One is that no matter how careful you are, at some point you or your employees are going to screw up in a way that affects your customer. Accept it and realize that it's what you do after you screw up that is more important.

These Shoes Feel Snug

Another lesson is a super old one and you've heard it before: Put yourself in your customer's shoes. It's a cliche, but it's also the magic behind every interaction you have. If you can imagine how you would feel and what you would want out of an unfortunate situation, then it will be much easier to figure out the right solution.

When you start from empathy and genuineness, you'll know what you need to do.

The problem isn't the problem. The problem is how you handle the problem.

Chapter Five

You Don't Need Another Policy (or any)

As your business grows and you hire more employees, it can be tempting to start creating a chain of policies so that everyone handles things in the same way when The Boss isn't around.

This is all very well, but a set of instructions on how to lock up at night is very different from interacting with customers. Don't confuse the two.

Don't hide behind policies when dealing with customers. Deal with people as people, not as if you were cleaning the yogurt machine. Every person and situation is different, even if they seem similar. At best, people bristle when quoted a policy. Don't do it.

But aren't some policies necessary? No, not when you're handling humans.

Let's say a customer drops a $100 bill to buy a $12 item, which leaves you short on cash to give change. A policy to only accept $100 bills on items over $50 solves that problem, but what if it's a $46 item? Then what?

It's not really about policies, it's about communicating with your customers in a genuine way. You could bluntly state, "Our policy is to not accept $100 bills."

Even if they know better than to try and make change like that, they'll think you are being difficult for no other reason than "policy," and they'll just feel put off.

A more communicative response would be, "I'm sorry, we can't accept a large bill like that. We won't be able to give change to our other customers."

They may be disappointed, but your explanation of how it affects other customers gives them the feeling that there's a practical reason, which is much easier to accept. Maybe they won't care anyway (we all know "that guy"), and we learn how to deal with those customers in a later chapter.

Policies are for locking up at night and washing your hands after using the bathroom. Leave the policies out of your customer interactions.

Chapter Six

(Don't) Do the Robot

Chain stores very often offer robotic experiences that lack warmth and connection to the customer. Much like the policy problems we talked about earlier, the high volume of traffic means that each guest is treated the same to make things more efficient.

Staples is a good (bad) example of the robot taking over. At some point, it seems the company made it policy to welcome each customer as they walk in the door. On the surface, this sounds like a great idea. After all, every customer should be welcomed, right?

In practice, it's at least an unpleasant experience, if not a downright disturbing one. When you walk in the door of a Staples, you hear "Welcome!" from someone in the checkout area, it's not always obvious who it was. It quickly becomes clear that it's not a genuine welcome, because you can't find anyone actually looking in your direction with a welcoming face. There's no chance to exchange the greeting because there's no one behind it. Everyone is heads-down at their register.

If you happen to be standing at checkout, you might experience your clerk suddenly shout "Welcome!" in the middle of your transaction, which is startling. Then they will go back to their task as if nothing happened.

This is not an example of human connection, it's merely employees following a script handed down by the corporate office. Customers can smell it from the front door. And though they may still run up to Staples to get their paper, they are probably not going to feel any sense of loyalty to the store. If a better sale or a great rewards program comes along somewhere else, they'll just go there instead.

You've probably heard some iteration of this at various stores when you shop. It's usually a bored, monotone utterance along the lines of "Hello-welcome-our-candles-are-50%-off-today."

It doesn't take much effort to toss out a robotic, scripted greeting. On the other hand, it doesn't really take any more effort to offer a warm, genuine greeting. It's kind of amazing how a tiny change can mean so much.

It's really as simple as saying, "Hi!" or "Hello, welcome!" as you would to a friend who comes to your home. You wouldn't smother them, or put on a syrupy-sweet facade for your friend, so treat your customers the same way. Be real. Be nice. Be present. Be helpful.

If It Bugs You Then...

Even though your business is small, there's still a lot you can learn from the big guys. When you shop, pay attention to those things that bug you. Chances are they are bugging other people, too. Yet unlike corporate chain stores, you have the ability to pivot and fix them quickly.

Chapter Seven

Hugging Your Customers

I've talked a lot about being warm and genuine with your customers. I hope that you're beginning to see that building your business for the long term is more about the experience people have with you than it is about sales and revenue. Those things are important, but your customers (people) come first. All revenue flows from those interactions and each one dictates how many more interactions you'll have in the future.

It's not about being a pushover, or even giving bear hugs to everyone who walks in the door. In fact, you probably shouldn't do that. The principle here is simple. When you show genuine care about the experience your customers have, they'll respond positively.

I Need to Speak to Carolina

A perfect example of this is a from a former co-worker of mine. At the consulting firm we worked in, we had dozens of clients calling in every day to get help with their presentations. Carolina, my co-worker, was a project coordinator who worked with our clients and then directed our in house team members to complete the work.

One client in particular (I'll call him Fernando) would call in and immediately ask to speak to Carolina. If she wasn't available, he would ask that she call him back so he could discuss his project.

We had other project coordinators and account relationship specialists who handled clients just as well, but none of them could talk to this client. He was cordial and professional, but firm. "I need to speak to

Carolina" was his mantra. At one point, Carolina went on vacation and sure enough, Fernando called in. He needed something urgently, but was firm that only Carolina would be able to handle it for him. He decided he could wait until she came back to get the help he needed.

What was going on? We were all competent professionals. Why Carolina? The answer is that she genuinely connected with him early on. She created an experience for him that was worth waiting for. The chances of him using another firm for his presentations were slim to none.

A caveat to this story is that it can be dangerous to have customers devoted to only one employee. If they leave, there's a risk of losing the customer. This is rare and you'll need to make sure there's a transition process with those customers.

Still, this is the situation you want to find yourself in with all your customers. You want to make such a connection early on that they can't imagine going anywhere else.

If You Fake It, You'll Never Be Satisfied

What if you're not a naturally smiley person? What if the thought of informal conversations with strangers terrifies you? Can you still give good service?

Of course you can. In fact, it's more important that you not try to fake a different personality. People can spot a phony and they'll react accordingly. When you're genuinely trying to be helpful, that will come through if you just act like yourself.

Giving good customer service is really about listening. If you take time to truly listen to a person, and you can offer a solution that shows you are aware and present, that's all you need to do.

You don't have to be Spongebob Squarepants to give good service. If you are polite and attentive, you don't have to go over the top to win people over.

The Customer Is Actually... Wrong?

The challenging customer. The grump. The chronic complainer. The uber picky one. We all have them. We've even been one at one time or another. These are the people who make you shake your fist at the phrase, "The customer is always right." The truth is, they're not always right and sometimes they are very, very wrong. And sometimes they will even treat you like garbage until they get what they want. They aren't fun. But, they are inevitable.

You can go crazy trying to make difficult people happy. They take up most of your time when your easy-to-please customers are gone too quickly. What can you do about them?

It's tempting to just get rid of them, tell them to ***k off and be done with the headache. It's pretty easy to just give them a refund and tell them to never come back. The danger is that, although emotionally satisfying for you, your most difficult customers tend to be your loudest customers. They will likely not go away quietly, rather, they will shout about their experience all over twitter and Yelp. And they will paint you as the villian.

A better strategy is empathy. Empathy is harder. It takes a lot of strength, but in the end you might find that the results are even more satisfying than the quicker solution of blowing them off. I learned this very early in my customer service career.

The Parable of the Pancake

One of my first jobs in high school was host at a pancake house. The job was easy enough. I only had to greet and seat customers and do some minimal cleaning around the host area. On slow weeknights, I could even get some homework done and eat free food. It was hard to believe that I actually got paid for it.

Weekends, on the other hand, were kind of a nightmare. We lived close to a retirement community in Phoenix, Arizona. On Sundays, we had a breakfast special for seniors. I can't say the food was anywhere near Michelin star-level, but on those days there was a line out the door. Combine the senior groups and the younger churchgoing family crowd and you are suddenly at PAN(cake)CON 1. Sometimes the wait for a table was an hour. Senior citizens like to feel special, very cared for. They also like to be seated immediately, not in an hour. We didn't take reservations, but that didn't stop many of them from treating it like brunch at The Plaza.

Complaints were many, they were swift, and they were often combined with a comment about my level of intelligence. "Is the corner booth ready? But we always eat at the corner booth. You should have kept it open for us. Can't you move them? Why not? What's a wheelchair table? Well, I guess I'll bring my wheelchair next time. Are you deaf? I hear better than you and I'm old. Hello? Are you deaf and dumb? Where's the manager?"

Every Sunday, the same complaints. The same grumps. The same challenge of trying to seat 200 people in a space with a capacity of 90. It seemed I could never do anything right for our guests, no matter how hard I tried. I certainly earned my money those days. Through it all I did my best to keep a smile and maintain foreign diplomat levels of politeness.

I wasn't always able to do that at first. I got outwardly frustrated at times. Then, after a particularly hard Sunday, my manager told me something. She explained that the oldsters weren't being difficult just to be mean. Many of them were living on very low incomes, sometimes their Social Security alone. They didn't exactly have money to burn. They also weren't living their best lives. They were often lonely, their friends were dying, some of them had no family around them. Many of them were battling chronic illnesses or just feeling their old age. So when Sunday comes, having breakfast at the local pancake house is exactly like brunch at The Plaza. They can afford to eat at a restaurant. They can socialize. They get treated nicely. We served a diner-style breakfast, but what were really giving them was dignity, a feeling of power and status, and a reason to keep going for another week.

When I used empathy and started seeing Sundays through their eyes, it was much easier to deal with the crowds. Little things, like having friendly chit chat with them while they waited, was all it took to keep them from getting ugly. When I recognized regulars, using their name as they came in made them feel like they were VIPs. They ate it up.

It turned things around for me, too. There were times when I would hear someone complain about the wait and a senior would quiet them down, saying, "They're doing the best they can, don't you see how busy it is today?" Instead of berating us, they became our champions.

Empathy was all it took to change both my view and their feeling of being treated well. There were still challenges, but for the most part the seniors were happy with our service.

You can incorporate this into your business as well. When dealing with a difficult customer, take a moment to understand where they're coming from and what they value. If it's too hard to figure out in a short time, ask. No kidding. Ask them about themselves, try to learn what they're looking to get out of the transaction. Is it just a slice of pizza, or is it a sense of community, or maybe even the one time they eat pizza all month? Start a conversation.

Save the Debates for an Election Year

Never debate or argue with a customer. You might want to tattoo that on your hand. Never, ever argue. You may be right in the end, but that's not the feeling they will take away. They will feel cheated, or just wronged and they won't be spreading good tidings about you and your business.

So what do you do when the customer really is wrong?

Remember in Chapter Four when you explained why you can't change a $100 bill? This is very similar. It takes a little explaining, but when you have facts you can demonstrate, many times the customer will appreciate it. Most situations where the customer is wrong come out of a misunderstanding. Whether it was at the beginning, middle or end of their experience, there was something they either didn't comprehend or wasn't communicated to them properly.

Sometimes a customer is not going to be satisfied even after you politely explain the misunderstanding. They're still going to have the feeling that something was wrong that didn't have anything to do with them. Even if, deep down, they know they were wrong, they won't want to hear it. The best thing you can do in those situations is to help the customer save face. One way to do that is by "hiring" them to help you solve the problem. Asking a question like, "How could we communicate this better in the future?" can help ease the pressure and help them feel that you're both in this together.

Born Angry

There will be times when you will deal with a person who simply wants to be angry about everything. No matter what you offer, no matter how politely you handle their experience, they just want to be mad. They probably got angry in the last place they shopped as well and it had nothing to do with their service, either. There will be times when you have done everything in your power to please them and it won't have any effect at all. Don't take it personally.

Some people believe that the only way to get anything in life is to shout or be aggressive. Their view is that businesses are out to cheat customers. They felt that way long before they met you and you had nothing to do with it.

The only thing you can do is continue to be polite and put it to them. What do they want? What will resolve their issue? They will probably have a specific answer. It may not be something you can give them on the spot. When that happens, you can get their information and promise to contact them with a resolution when you've had some time to think it over or talk to your boss. If you are the boss, then you may need time to think it over and you absolutely have the right to do that.

Don't let it rattle you. It's going to happen sooner or later and when it does, you'll be even better prepared the next time.

Chapter Nine

Putting It All Together

We've talked about a lot of different situations and strategies to handle them. Strategies or tactics aside, I hope you're getting an understanding that underneath all of that stuff is the core philosophy that you are in service to people. You can follow the advice in this book and I hope it's helpful. If you get anything out of it, I hope that you take away the idea that no matter what situation you find yourself in, you need to realize that your only job is to help your customer.

This is why it doesn't matter a whole lot if you are introverted or not super peppy like a Tupperware hostess. It really is fine. People want to deal with other people who are being themselves. If you don't put on an act and you only seek to help them get what they need, you'll be doing the right thing for them and your business.

Santa Claus, Marketing Genius

In the 1947 film Miracle on 34th Street, the store Santa Claus starts sending customers to other stores when Macy's doesn't have what they were shopping for. Initially, the store manager freaks out, but then comes to realize that sending customers elsewhere is actually creating more loyal customers. Even today, it's still a controversial idea for big box and chain stores. It's too much for those large businesses to trust their front-facing employees to do what's best for the situation, which is why they feel they need to have so many policies in place.

The temptation is to keep as much business to yourself and fear similar businesses as The Evil Competition. When you go out of your way to help someone get what they need, even when it's not with you, they will remember you and think well of your business. They may even send friends to you when they have the opportunity. It's the difference between saying, "We don't do that" and "Let's figure out how you can get it." It's really that simple.

The Long Game

Like we've discussed before, great customer service is about the long game. The short game is about individual money-making transactions, but that doesn't help you grow. If you want to keep your business healthy for years to come, you need to make every interaction a legitimate transaction, whether it puts money in the register or not. In fact, every time you answer a question, every time you interact on social media, you are conducting business. You create customers long before money changes hands.

People Who Need People

You started your business with the intent to make it succeed (at least I hope you did, because the alternative is really weird). And that's amazing, the act of creating something out of nothing to provide for yourself, your family and the community you want to serve. To realize that dream takes a lot of work and tons of courage. Kudos to you! Don't get so caught up in the money that you forget that it's about the people. Customers are people and you need people to exist. I just said "people" a lot but it's important. They are numero uno. When you put your focus on them, you can't help but provide the best service and your business will grow.

Go be of service to your people. They need your help.

About the Author

D.J. Billings has been a professional illustrator and animator for over twenty years. D.J.'s clients have included MTV Networks, Highlights Magazine, Sesame Workshop, and Nickelodeon.

D.J. has written and published four books (and counting).

Along with wife Jenni, D.J. also run Sparky Firepants Screen Printing, an apparel decorating and design studio.

They live in Los Angeles with their children, pets and a 1966 VW Beetle named Helga.

Get in touch! Email: dj@itsjustdj.com